2016

SEATTLE SEAHAWKS

BY TYLER MASON

SportsZone

An Imprint of Abdo Publishing
abdopublishing.com

abdopublishing.com

Published by Abdo Publishing, a division of ABDO, PO Box 398166, Minneapolis, Minnesota 55439. Copyright © 2017 by Abdo Consulting Group, Inc. International copyrights reserved in all countries. No part of this book may be reproduced in any form without written permission from the publisher. SportsZone™ is a trademark and logo of Abdo Publishing.

Printed in the United States of America, North Mankato, Minnesota
042016
092016

Cover Photo: Damian Strohmeyer/AP Images
Interior Photos: Damian Strohmeyer/AP Images, 1 ; Paul Sancya/AP Images, 4-5; Kathy Willens/ AP Images, 6; Ted S. Warren/AP Images, 6-7; Vernon Biever/AP Images, 8-9; Al Messerschmidt/ AP Images, 10-11; AP Images, 12-13; Gary Stewart, 14-15; Greg Trott/AP Images, 16, 26-27; Kevin Terrell/NFL Photos/AP Images, 17; Al Golub/AP Images, 18-19; Rick Bowmer/AP Images, 20-21; David Drapkin/AP Images, 22-23; Ross D. Franklin/AP Images, 24; Denis Poroy/AP Images, 25; Scott Boehm/AP Images, 28-29.

Editor: Patrick Donnelly
Series Designer: Nikki Farinella

Cataloging-in-Publication Data
Names: Mason, Tyler, author.
Title: Seattle Seahawks / by Tyler Mason.
Description: Minneapolis, MN : Abdo Publishing, [2017] | Series: NFL up close |
    Includes index.
Identifiers: LCCN 2015960451 | ISBN 9781680782332 (lib. bdg.) |
    ISBN 9781680776447 (ebook)
Subjects: LCSH: Seattle Seahawks (Football team)--History--Juvenile
    literature. | National Football League--Juvenile literature. | Football--Juvenile
    literature. | Professional sports--Juvenile literature. | Football teams--
    Washington (State)--Juvenile literature.
Classification: DDC 796.332--dc23
LC record available at http://lccn.loc.gov/2015960451

TABLE OF CONTENTS

WORLD CHAMPIONS

The Seattle Seahawks had the best defense in the National Football League (NFL) in 2013. The Denver Broncos had scored more points than any team in NFL history that year. Something had to give when they met in the Super Bowl.

The game was filled with big plays, and most of them went Seattle's way. Right away, a bad snap sent the football skittering past Broncos quarterback Peyton Manning and into the end zone. The Broncos fell on it, but Seattle was awarded a safety. The Seahawks led 2-0 just 12 seconds into the Super Bowl.

Peyton Manning, *18*, chases the football after it was snapped past him for a safety in the Super Bowl against the Seahawks.

That play set the tone for the game. Seattle also scored on a 69-yard interception return by linebacker Malcolm Smith in the first half. Percy Harvin returned the second-half kickoff for a touchdown. Quarterback Russell Wilson threw two touchdown passes. On offense, defense, and special teams, the Seahawks could not be stopped.

Seattle's 43-8 win was the first Super Bowl victory in Seahawks history, a span of nearly 40 years. The players dumped a bucket of Gatorade over coach Pete Carroll. Team owner Paul Allen accepted the Lombardi Trophy. And three days later, nearly 1 million fans packed the streets of Seattle to celebrate the city's first Super Bowl.

Seahawks quarterback Russell Wilson discusses strategy with coach Pete Carroll.

Percy Harvin runs away from the pack as he returns a kickoff for a touchdown against the Denver Broncos in the Super Bowl.

FAST FACT

Malcolm Smith was named the Super Bowl Most Valuable Player (MVP). In addition to his touchdown, Smith recovered a fumble and had six tackles.

Quarterback Jim Zorn feels the heat from the Green Bay Packers pass rush in a 1976 game.

SEAHAWKS TAKE FLIGHT

People in Seattle had talked about building a domed sports stadium for nearly 20 years. Those talks finally became a reality in the mid-1970s. King County taxpayers agreed to build the Kingdome in 1972. When the NFL decided to expand by two teams, one of them went to Seattle.

More than 1,700 names were suggested for the new team. The Seahawks played their first NFL season in 1976, the same year the Kingdome opened. It was a rough start for the expansion team. The Seahawks finished 2-12 in their first year.

FAST FACT

Steve Niehaus became the first Seattle Seahawk in 1976. Seattle drafted him from Notre Dame. Niehaus was a defensive lineman. He played in four NFL seasons.

The Seahawks' first quarterback was Jim Zorn. He was a rookie in 1976. Zorn was a left-handed passer who could throw well on the run. He quickly developed a connection with wide receiver Steve Largent that would serve them well over the years.

Seattle's first regular-season win came on October 17, 1976. The Seahawks beat the other new expansion team, the Tampa Bay Buccaneers, 13-10. The Seahawks won only one more game in their first season. Zorn threw two touchdown passes in a 30-13 win over the Atlanta Falcons.

The Kingdome was the Seahawks' home until 2000.

FAST FACT

The Kingdome also was home to Major League Baseball's Seattle Mariners. The National Basketball Association's Seattle SuperSonics also played there for seven seasons.

Seahawks players carry Chuck Knox off the field after they upset the Miami Dolphins in the 1983 AFC playoffs.

FEAST AND FAMINE

The Seahawks made the playoffs for the first time in 1983. It was their first year under coach Chuck Knox, who had turned the Los Angeles Rams into a powerhouse a decade earlier. Jim Zorn shared the quarterback duties with Dave Krieg. Each player started eight games that season. The Seahawks finished 9-7 and earned a wild-card berth in the American Football Conference (AFC) playoffs.

Then the playoff newcomers went on a run. The Seahawks crushed the Denver Broncos 31-7 in the first round. Then they shocked the top-seeded Miami Dolphins with a 27-20 upset on the road. Finally, the Los Angeles Raiders ended their roll with a 30-14 win in the AFC Championship Game.

13

The Seahawks proved that their 1983 success was no accident. They went to the postseason four times in six years between 1983 and 1988. They even got revenge on the Raiders, beating them in the first round in 1984.

Soon after, Seattle had a decade of tough times. The Seahawks missed the playoffs every season from 1989 to 1998. They cycled through three coaches in that time. In 1992, Knox was replaced by Tom Flores. He had won two Super Bowls with the Raiders. But after just three seasons, the Seahawks turned to Dennis Erickson. He had won two national championships at the University of Miami. Erickson was not able to get the Seahawks to the Super Bowl.

Steve Largent, *80*, was the NFL career leader with 100 touchdown catches when he retired.

FAST FACT

Steve Largent held six NFL career receiving records when he retired in 1989. He was inducted into the Pro Football Hall of Fame in 1995.

Finally, Mike Holmgren came to town in 1999. Holmgren had turned around the Green Bay Packers and led them to a Super Bowl title in the 1996 season. In Seattle, he inherited a team that included two future Hall of Famers: tackle Walter Jones and defensive lineman Cortez Kennedy. Running back Ricky Watters was in the midst of a six-year streak of 1,000-yard rushing seasons. And linebacker Chad Brown was a first-team All-Pro selection in 1998.

Holmgren took that talented roster and built a winner in Seattle.

Tackle Walter Jones anchored the Seattle offensive line from 1997 through 2008.

Cortez Kennedy was named to the Pro Bowl eight times in his 11 seasons with the Seahawks.

SUPER BOWL BOUND

Mike Holmgren worked quickly. He led Seattle to the AFC playoffs in 1999. Two years later, he brought quarterback Matt Hasselbeck to Seattle. Hasselbeck had been Brett Favre's backup for the Green Bay Packers. He teamed with Holmgren to get the Seahawks to the Super Bowl in 2005.

They got a lot of help from Shaun Alexander, too. The running back led the NFL with 1,880 yards and 28 total touchdowns in 2005. It was his fifth straight 1,000-yard season and a career year for the hard-charging running back. He ended up winning the NFL MVP Award that season.

FAST FACT

The Seahawks switched conferences in 2002. The NFL wanted the expansion Houston Texans to play in the AFC, so Seattle moved to the National Football Conference (NFC).

In 2005, Shaun Alexander became the first Seahawk to be named MVP of the NFL.

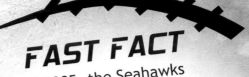

FAST FACT
In 2005, the Seahawks led the NFL in points scored for the first time in team history.

The Seahawks finished the 2005 regular season with a 13-3 record. It was the best record in the NFC. That meant they would not have to leave Seattle to earn a trip to the Super Bowl. Their hometown fans roared their approval.

The Seahawks beat Washington 20-10 in their first playoff game. Then they blew out the Carolina Panthers 34-14 in the NFC Championship Game.

Seattle quarterback Matt Hasselbeck scampers into the end zone during the Seahawks' playoff victory against Washington.

21

The Seahawks faced the Pittsburgh Steelers in the Super Bowl. They fell behind just before halftime and never regained the lead. Seattle was called for seven penalties in the 21-10 loss. Many Seahawks fans were angry afterward. They thought the officials made several calls that changed the game. The head referee later admitted that he missed two important calls in the fourth quarter.

Seahawks coach Mike Holmgren spent much of the Super Bowl asking for explanations of the officials' calls.

FAST FACT

Mike Holmgren was the Seahawks' coach for 10 seasons. He finished his time in Seattle with an 86-74 record. Through 2015, he had the most wins of any Seahawks coach.

BACK-TO-BACK?

Seattle went to the playoffs four times in between Super Bowl appearances but never got past the second round. Pete Carroll arrived in 2010 to coach the team. He had been a big success at the University of Southern California. The Seahawks drafted Russell Wilson in 2012. He surprised everyone by winning the starting quarterback job as a rookie. Wilson led them to the playoffs in his first year and the Super Bowl the next.

Then, after beating the Denver Broncos to win the Super Bowl, the Seahawks had another incredible season. Seattle went 12-4 in 2014 and took on the New England Patriots in the Super Bowl.

Seahawks quarterback Russell Wilson takes the snap against the Arizona Cardinals in his first NFL game.

Cornerback Richard Sherman is a key member of the "Legion of Boom."

It was a tight game throughout. Wilson threw a touchdown pass to wide receiver Doug Baldwin late in the third quarter to put Seattle on top 24-14. But the Patriots came roaring back in the fourth quarter. New England scored two touchdowns to go ahead 28-24 with just over two minutes remaining.

Seattle still had a chance to win. Wilson drove the Seahawks to the New England 1-yard line with 26 seconds left. But instead of using hard-hitting running back Marshawn Lynch to pound the ball into the end zone, Seattle decided to pass. Patriots cornerback Malcolm Butler jumped in front of Wilson's pass and made a game-saving interception. New England won 28-24.

Marshawn Lynch, 24, bursts through a big hole in the New England defensive line during the Super Bowl in February 2015.

FAST FACT

Seahawks fans are called the "12th Man" or simply "12s." Their loud cheering at home games makes it seem as though Seattle has an extra player on the field.

FAST FACT

Russell Wilson set an NFL record on October 19, 2014. He became the first quarterback to throw for 300 yards and rush for 100 yards in the same game.

The Seahawks made the playoffs again in 2015 but did not advance to their third straight Super Bowl. Lynch retired after the season, but with Wilson and a strong defense in place, the Seahawks were in position to be an NFC power for years to come.

Russell Wilson scrambles away from a Carolina Panthers defender during a playoff game in January 2016.

TIMELINE

1976
The Seattle Seahawks play their first NFL season.

1983
Seattle makes the postseason for the first time with a 9-7 record.

1984
The team retires the No. 12 in honor of the fans, who are known as the "12th Man."

1989
Hall of Fame wide receiver Steve Largent retires after 14 seasons.

1999
Mike Holmgren takes over as the sixth head coach in team history.

2002
On September 15, Seattle plays its first game at Seahawks Stadium, later known as Qwest Field and CenturyLink Field.

2006
The Seahawks make it to their first Super Bowl but lose to the Pittsburgh Steelers 21-10 on February 5.

2008
After reaching the playoffs five straight seasons, the Seahawks go 4-12 and Holmgren retires.

2010
The Seahawks hire coach Pete Carroll, a former championship-winning coach at the University of Southern California.

2014
On February 2, Seattle wins its first Super Bowl, defeating the Denver Broncos 43-8.

2015
The Seahawks appear in their second straight Super Bowl but lose to the New England Patriots 28-24 on February 1.

GLOSSARY

COORDINATOR
An assistant coach who is in charge of a team's offense or defense.

DIVISION
A group of teams that help form a league.

DOMED
Having a roof.

INTERCEPTION
When a defensive player catches a pass intended for an offensive player.

SAFETY
A score of two points for a team when its opponent is unable to advance the ball out of its own end zone.

SNAP
The start of each play, when the center hikes the ball between his legs to a player behind him, usually the quarterback.

SPECIAL TEAMS
The players on the field for kicking and punting plays.

WILD CARD
A team that makes the playoffs even though it did not win its division.

INDEX

ABOUT THE AUTHOR

Tyler Mason studied journalism at the University of Wisconsin. He has covered professional and college sports in Minneapolis and St. Paul, Minnesota, since 2009. He currently lives in Hudson, Wisconsin, with his wife.